Walk Around

B-52 Stratofortress

By Lou Drendel

Walk Around Number 6

squadron/signal publications

Introduction

It is one of the most long-lived of combat aircraft, having first flown over forty years ago. But it is not only longevity that makes the B-52 noteworthy. It is still one of the largest aircraft in the world, with a length of over 160 feet, a wingspan of 185 feet, a height of 48 feet, and a gross weight of almost a half a million pounds! It made the first around-world-nonstop flight of a turbojet powered aircraft, circling the globe in 45 hours, 19 minutes, during 1957. Twenty-three years later, it made the fastest non-stop around-the-world flight, in 42 hours, 23 minutes. In 1962, it held the record for the longest unrefueled flight, a staggering 11,337 miles! It holds the record for the largest bomb load, 70,000 pounds. And, for the record, it is the oldest operational combat aircraft in the U.S. inventory. While carrying the badge of the now defunct Strategic Air Command, the B-52 was the big stick which enabled SAC to live up to it's motto; "Peace Is Our Profession." Peace was their profession and their goal. They were a major deterrent force and ultimately one of the winning instruments of the cold war victory. But, when they had to fight in conventional wars, their bomb-carrying capability made them devastating weapons. Now in the fifth decade of operational service, the B-52 is still a formidable airplane, and this old soldier is not destined to fade away very soon.

Acknowledgements

Boeing
NASA
Douglas Olson
USAF
Ted Carlson-Fotodynamics
Ken Buchanan

COPYRIGHT 1996 SQUADRON/SIGNAL PUBLICATIONS, INC.
1115 CROWLEY DRIVE CARROLLTON, TEXAS 75011-5010
All rights reserved. No part of this publication may be reproduced, stored in a retrieval system or transmitted in any form by means electrical, mechanical or otherwise, without written permission of the publisher.

ISBN 0-89747-358-2

If you have any photographs of aircraft, armor, soldiers or ships of any nation, particularly wartime snapshots, why not share them with us and help make Squadron/Signal's books all the more interesting and complete in the future. Any photograph sent to us will be copied and the original returned. The donor will be fully credited for any photos used. Please send them to:

Squadron/Signal Publications, Inc.
1115 Crowley Drive
Carrollton, TX 75011-5010

Если у вас есть фотографии самолётов, вооружения, солдат или кораблей любой страны, особенно, снимки времён войны, поделитесь с нами и помогите сделать новые книги издательства Эскадрон/Сигнал ещё интереснее. Мы переснимем ваши фотографии и вернём оригиналы. Имена приславших снимки будут сопровождать все опубликованные фотографии. Пожалуйста, присылайте фотографии по адресу:

Squadron/Signal Publications, Inc.
1115 Crowley Drive
Carrollton, TX 75011-5010

軍用機、装甲車両、兵士、軍艦などの写真を所持しておられる方はいらっしゃいませんか？どの国のものでも結構です。作戦中に撮影されたものが特に良いのです。Squadron/Signal社の出版する刊行物において、このような写真は内容を一層充実し、興味深くすることができます。当方にお送り頂いた写真は、複写の後お返しいたします。出版物中に写真を使用した場合は、必ず提供者のお名前を明記させて頂きます。お写真は下記にご送付ください。

Squadron/Signal Publications, Inc.
1115 Crowley Drive
Carrollton, TX 75011-5010

The first Stratofortress was the XB-52; which was rolled out on 29 November 1951. Damaged during ground tests, the XB-52 did not fly until 2 October 1952. In the meantime, the YB-52 made the first flight on 15 April 1952. Legendary Boeing test pilot A.M. "Tex" Johnson was in the cockpit. (USAF)

The B-52A made its first flight on 5 August 1954. A total of three B-52As were built at an average cost of just over $29 million each. The balance of the original order for thirteen B-52As were built as B-52Bs. (Boeing)

The sixth production B-52, a B-52B, was built with a reconnaissance capability, giving it the official designation of RB-52B. Most of that capability was built into a two-man capsule; which was carried in the bomb bay. These crewmen were able to perform electronic countermeasures and/or photographic reconnaissance. They were provided with downward firing ejection seats. Unit cost on the fifty B-52Bs was $7.3 million. (Boeing)

170 B-52Ds were built. This B-52D has a GAM-72 Quail decoy missile on a trailer along side of it. The Quail was powered by a single J-85 engine and built by McDonnell. Production efficiencies continued to mount as B-52 production accelerated, bringing the unit cost down further to $4.1 million. (USAF)

100 B-52Es were built, forty-two in Seattle and fifty-eight in Wichita. The B-52E was the first B-52 equipped for low altitude penetration of enemy defenses. (Boeing)

102 B-52Hs were built, all in Wichita. The B-52H was the last variant of the B-52 to be delivered, beginning in May 1961. The addition of more electronic gear and newer turbo-fan engines resulted in an initial unit cost of $6.8 million. (Ken Buchanan)

The B-52G and B-52H were the only B-52 variants to receive a number of modifications to make them more effective bombers and to enhance their survivability. Most of these modifications are evidenced by the added antennas on the fuselage, nose, and tail. (Ted Carlson)

The B-52G and B-52H were modified with a number of new avionics/electronics systems; which are evidenced by the added antennas on the nose. The hydraulically-operated air refuelling slipway doors on the fuselage spine are open, showing the refueling receptacle. All of the B-52s tanks can be filled from this single point. The rate of fuel flow is controlled by the tanker crew and by the number of receiver tanks open. There are switches which sense when a tank is full, both by weight and volume, and will operate valves to shut off flow to that tank. The B-52 was equipped with wind shield wipers on the windows in front of both the pilot and co-pilot's positions. (Ted Carlson)

A B-52H of the 410th Bomb Wing, K.I. Sawyer Air Force Base, Michigan, during the Summer of 1994. The large bullet fairings on the sides of the nose cover three antennas for the ALQ-117 Electronic Countermeasures (ECM) system. The small blade antenna just behind the radome is for the Radar Bombing Navigation System. The Black silhouette represents the upper peninsula of Michigan, with a star indicating the location of K.I. Sawyer AFB.

A B-52F (serial 57-0037A) in typical SAC markings: Natural Metal uppersurfaces, nuclear blast reflective Gloss White undersurfaces. The B-52F was the last of the tall tail B-52s. It featured the more powerful J57-P-43 engines; which would also power the B-52G. (Douglas Olson)

B-52D Stratofortress

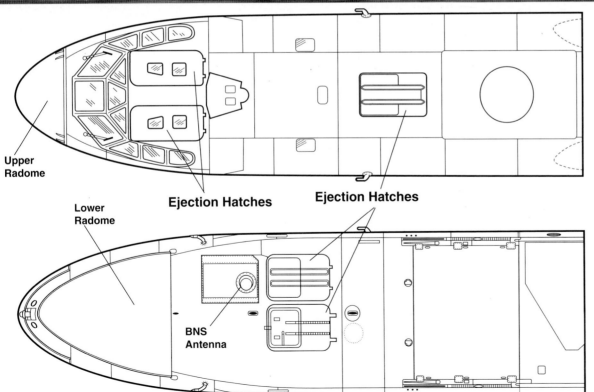
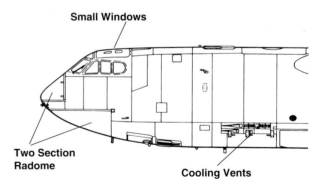

The early B-52D was a sleek aircraft. One of the most notable characteristics of the B-52's long, tapered wings was the very evident wing flex (up or down, according to wing loading). (Boeing)

B-52D

B-52F

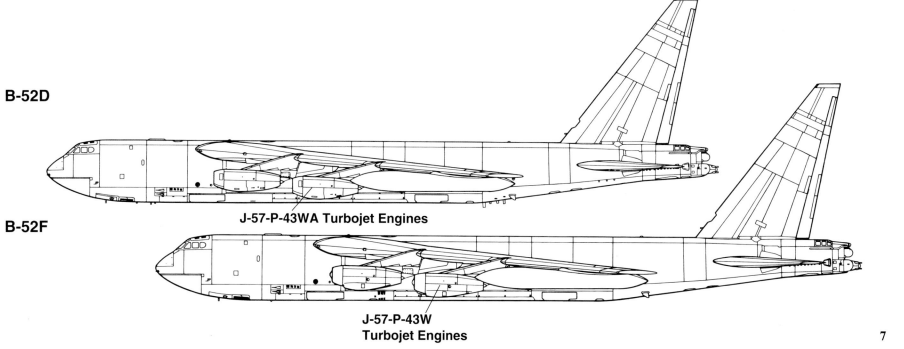

J-57-P-43WA Turbojet Engines

J-57-P-43W Turbojet Engines

The large fairing on top of the radome covers the ALT-28 ECM Jammer antenna. The radome itself covers the AN/ALR-20A Strategic Radar System. The EVS turrets have both been hand-rotated to show the sensor windows (normally, the turrets would be in the stowed position when on the ground).

This B-52-GR (60-030) of the 416th Bomb Wing at Nellis AFB, NV, on 18 October 1993, for the Gunsmoke Bombing Competition was named "Miss Liberty." The EVS turrets are in the stowed, protected position. (Ted Carlson-Fotodynamics)

A B-52G-ED (80235) of the 412th Test Wing, 419th Test Squadron at Edwards AFB, CA on 23 October 1993. The avionics and electronic components carried by the current generation of B-52s require extensive cooling scoops and vents. (Ted Carlson-Fotodynamics)

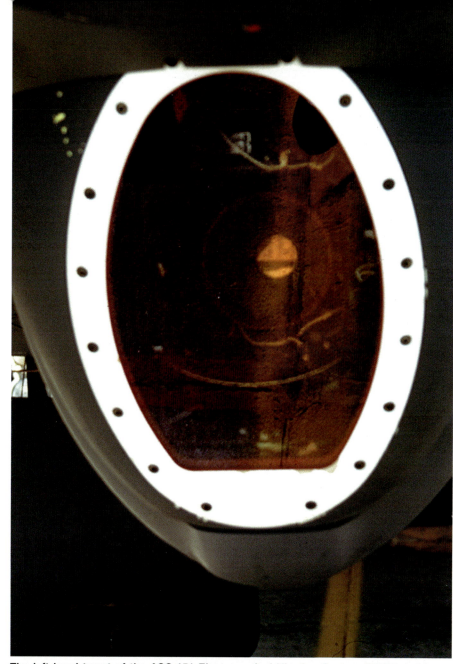

The left hand turret of the ASQ-151 Electro-optical Viewing System (EVS) contains a Westinghouse low-light level TV system. The turret is steerable and its images are projected on the CRT on the pilots and/or co-pilots instrument panel.

The right hand turret contains the Hughes Forward Looking Infrared (FLIR) system, whose images are also projected on cockpit CRTs. The turrets can be rotated 45 degrees left or right. They are rotated 180 degrees for storage to protect the sensor windows while not in use. The TV window is clear, while the FLIR window is mirror-glazed germanium.

B-52G/H EVS modifications were begun during 1972. By 1974, at least one B-52G at Barksdale AFB, LA, had not been modified showing the profile differences between a modified aircraft (left) and unmodified variant (right). (USAF)

A brand-new B-52H shortly after roll out at the Boeing Wichita plant. It is carrying four prototype GAM-87 Skybolt missiles, which were designed as stand off weapons. These missiles had a range of from 600 to 1,000 miles, depending upon warhead weight. The Skybolt program was cancelled by President Kennedy during 1962. (Boeing)

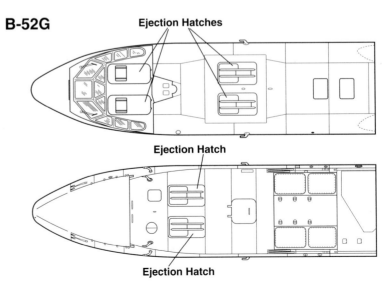

B-52G

Ejection Hatches

Ejection Hatch

Ejection Hatch

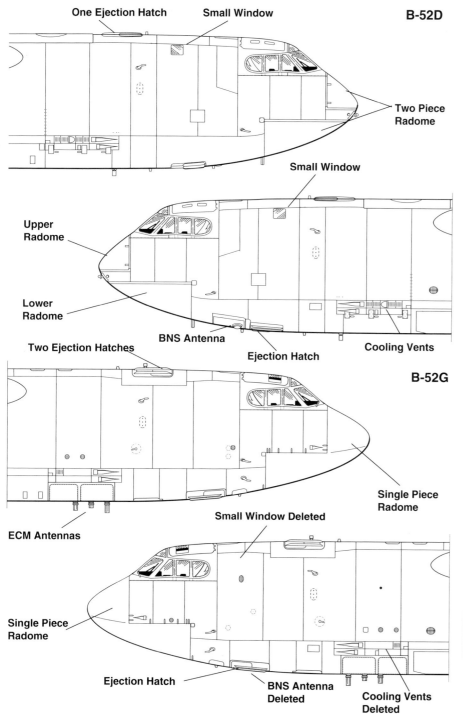

B-52D

- One Ejection Hatch
- Small Window
- Two Piece Radome

- Upper Radome
- Lower Radome
- Small Window
- BNS Antenna
- Ejection Hatch
- Cooling Vents

B-52G

- Two Ejection Hatches
- ECM Antennas
- Single Piece Radome

- Single Piece Radome
- Ejection Hatch
- Small Window Deleted
- BNS Antenna Deleted
- Cooling Vents Deleted

A recently-modified clean EVS-equipped B-52G. There are seven ECM blade antennas visible to the rear of the open crew access hatch. (USAF)

The right side of the nose mounts the pitot static tube (lower) and the angle of attack sensor (top). There is an ejection seat warning immediately above the hatch for the Radar Navigator's downward-firing ejection seat.

EVS turrets and fairing on a B-52H at K.I. Sawyer AFB during July of 1994. The EVS is fully integrated with the Norden Systems strategic radar, including the ASG-21 radar fire control system. Each crewmember can select either TV or FLIR, independent of each other, for viewing on their CRTs. The pilots have a steering priority system to ensure that they can override other commands, making certain they get the appropriate views during low level missions.

The forward fuselage of this B-52H shows considerable skin wrinkling, the result of the accumulated stress of thousands of hours of peacekeeping over a thirty three year span. No major structural changes were made to the basic B-52 fuselage when the B-52G and B-52H models were introduced.

This is the main external ground power unit connections. The B-52 requires three connections for 205 volt three phase a-c power, and one 24 volt d-c connection. There are two other external power receptacles, one for the bombing navigational system, and a third for the gunnery system.

The main external power receptacle has seven pins. In addition to the four previously mentioned, one is not used, and two serve as grounds. The controls for the external power receptacle are located in the cockpit.

The wing anhedral on this B-52G is evident without air loads. The major modifications from B-52F to B-52G included a weight savings of over 15,000 pounds, primarily through a reduction in the height of the vertical stabilizer, elimination of the pressurized tail gunner's compartment and a redesign of the wings. (Boeing)

B-52G

B-52G Phase IV

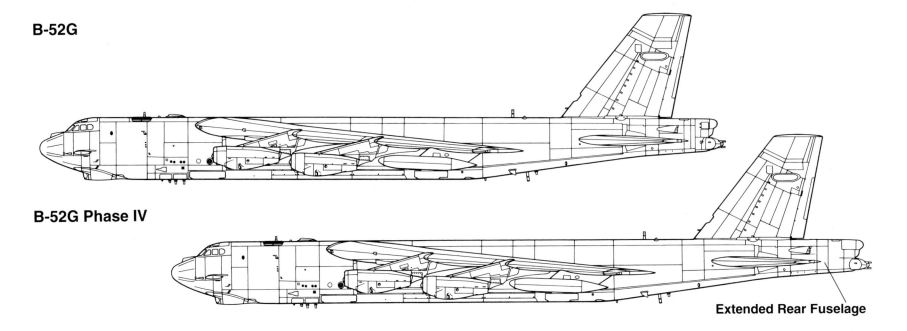

Extended Rear Fuselage

This is a lightly loaded (the wingtip landing gear is well clear of the ground) B-52G. The B-52G was the first B-52 to use integral fuel tanks (a "wet wing"). Internal fuel capacity was 46,576 gallons, with smaller 1,400 gallon underwing tanks. Unrefueled range of the B-52G was 400 miles more than the earlier B-52F.

A six man crew from the 456th Aerospace Wing scrambles to get their B-52 airborne. Drills like these were all too common during the cold war, and provided the deterrent that kept the war from becoming terminally hot. (USAF)

Installation of the EVS pre-dated the addition of more sophisticated ECM equipment on B-52Gs and B-52Hs. The EVS windows can be washed in flight (while in the stowed position) up to nine times with 160 degree pre-heated water, sprayed at 500 psi. (Boeing)

This B-52H (59-2592); which like most USAF aircraft, carried standard Southeast Asia camouflage colors during the Vietnam War. Nose art was accepted during bombing competitions, but not in regular squadron service. (Ken Buchanan)

The main landing gear of the B-52 consists of four fuselage-mounted, steerable double wheel main mounts. Landing gear retraction is forward, up, and inboard for the left gear, aft, up and inboard for the right gear.

Nose art returned with a vengeance during the late 1980s, culminating with Operation DESERT STORM. A lot of Second World War bomber nose art was resurrected, including this classic, used on a B-52H (0045) of the 92nd Bomb Wing. (Ted Carlson-Fotodynamics)

The bottom of the fuselage is studded with antennas, most of which are for the many and varied ECM systems necessary to protect an aircraft with a huge radar cross section.

A B-52G in the pre-contact position for a post-DESERT STORM mission refueling. Over eighty B-52s participated in DESERT STORM, operating from bases in England, Spain, Diego Garcia, Egypt, and Saudi Arabia. They were credited with demoralizing the Iraqi Republican Guard troops prior to the start of the ground war. (USAF)

B-52H

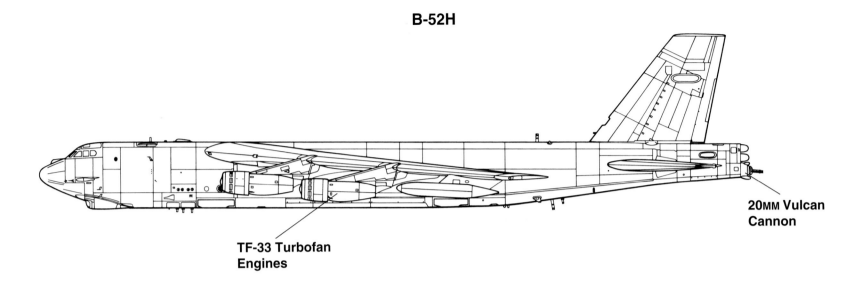

TF-33 Turbofan Engines

20MM Vulcan Cannon

A B-52H rolls out after landing at Biggs Army Airfield, Texas during Exercise Busy Prairie II, in June of 1981. The forty-four foot ribbon type drag chute is fully deployed. The drag chute is normally used on every landing and is deployed just after landing, above 90 knots. Deployment time is four seconds after pulling the handle; which opens the door and pulls the ripcord. All seven spoilers on the top of each wing are fully deployed to "dump lift" and make the anti-skid braking system more effective. (USAF)

A B-52H flies over Egypt during Exercise Bright Star 83. The wing sweep is 35 degrees and the span is 185 feet, with an aspect ratio of 8.56 and area of 4,000 square feet. By way of comparison, the average two story home is less than 3,000 square feet! The wing chord is 30 feet 11 inches at the root and 12 feet 4 inches at the tip. (USAF)

The top forward fuselage of a B-52H. The large bulged in the foreground is the Astro Navigation Antenna and above it is a small blade antenna. The side-by-side escape/ejection hatches for the Gunner and Electronic Warfare Officer are visible at top.

The two Gray lines running down the length of the upper fuselage spine are the fuselage walkway. There are numerous sensor covers and fuel filler covers along the fuselage spine.

Ejection/escape hatch covers for the Gunner and Electronic Warfare Officer have stiffeners to enhance structural stability. They are also equipped with jettison thrusters to provide positive separation from the aircraft during the ejection sequence.

This is the fuselage fuel tank probe receptacle. This fuel cell holds 6,791 gallons of jet fuel. The service markings are in Light Gray.

This is the outboard wing tank exterior filler cap. This fuel tank holds 1,148 gallons of fuel.

Looking aft along the top of the B-52H fuselage toward the vertical stabilizer. The fuselage is 160 feet 10 inches long.

21

This four blade antenna "tree" (looking forward) is located on top of the rear fuselage between the fuselage walkway stripes.

The same antenna "tree", looking aft. It is a C-band, winged four blade for the ALQ-122/ALT-16A, system 9. The dome on the walkway stripe is a anti-collision light (Red). There is a second light placed on the opposite walkway stripe.

A large ram air scoop is located at the base of the vertical fin for cooling the components of the ECM equipment in the aft equipment bay.

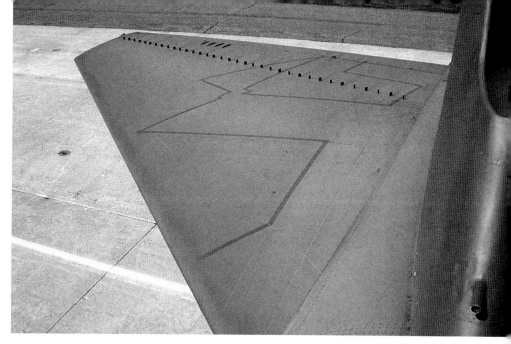

The starboard (above) and port (below) horizontal stabilizers. The walkway markings are different on the stabilizers. A row of vortex generators behind the mid-point of the stabilizer increases the effectiveness of the elevators on the trailing edges. The tail surfaces span fifty-two feet. The stabilizers pivot through four feet of travel to allow for trim control. The elevators are only seventy-nine square feet and do not have enough authority to overcome incorrect positioning of the stabilizers. The horizontal stabilizers are identical on all models of the B-52.

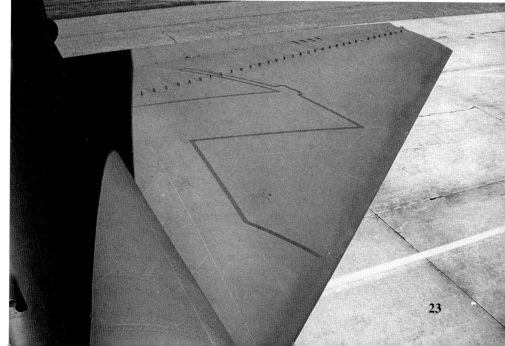

There are fifty vortex generators on the top of the port wing of the B-52H. The circle at center is a fuel tank filler cap.

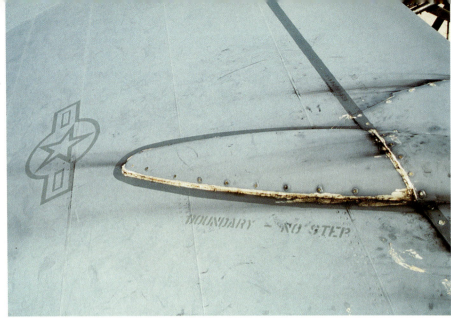

The rear of the outboard engine mounting pylon on the top of the port wing. It is designated as a "NO STEP" area and properly marked.

B-52s which are equipped to carry Air Launched Cruise Missiles (ALCMs) have a row of thirty-one vortex generators applied to the leading edge of the wings between the inboard engine plyon and the fuselage.

The B-52G and B-52H have no ailerons, roll control being provided by spoilers located on top of the wings. There are seven spoilers on each wing, each having its own hydraulically operated actuator. The three inboard spoilers are interconnected and operate as one unit. The four outboard spoilers are also interconnected and operate as one unit. Control wheel travel of 80° will give full extension of the spoilers. Extension of the spoilers on one wing decreases the lift on that wing, causing it to rotate downward, producing a rolling movement in that direction. The addition of drag also causes a yawing movement in that direction, assisting in coordination of the turn. The spoilers are also used as airbrakes, and can be raised to various positions. Application of left or right "stick" will cause raising or lowering of the spoilers to accommodate the roll rate called for by control inputs. Above 250 knots, the spoiler actuators do not have enough power to overcome airloads for full extension. As speeds increase, the available amount of spoiler extension goes down. At maximum airspeed, only 20° of the spoilers are available.

The inner three and outer four spoilers operate differentially. Spoilers do not cause any appreciable amount of buffet, even when deployed at high speeds, although the B-52 flight manual cautions against deployment of the spoilers to position 6 (full open) at air speeds in excess of 305 knots Indicated Air Speed (IAS).

B-52 Wing

All B-52 models use the same basic wing with a span of 185 feet and an area of 4,000 square feet. The wing is a high aspect, shoulder mounted, tapered design. Beginning with the B-52G, the wing became a integral fuel tank or "wet" wing, greatly increasing the fuel capacity and range.

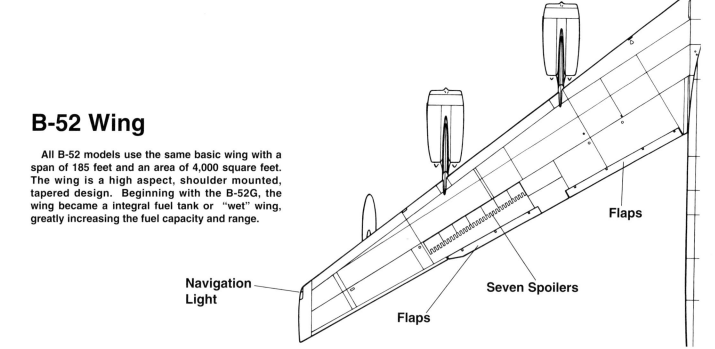

Simultaneous deployment of flaps and spoilers does not affect the aircraft's roll control appreciably. The flaps are so designed that the highest lift-drag ratio is achieved at the 100% down position. For this reason, the flaps are always used in the full down position.

Full extension of the flaps requires one minute, and they are ineffective in the intermediate positions. The flaps provide 797 square feet of control surface and are constructed of aluminum alloy frames with bonded aluminum alloy skins.

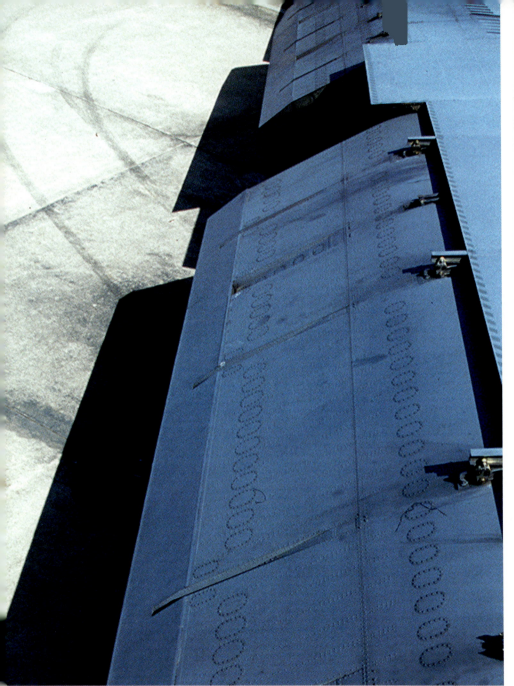

The flaps rotate downward thirty-five feet with little rearward movement. 'The balance of the 37.5 foot extension is downward, although most of the drag occurs within the first 20% of flap extension; which takes twelve seconds. The flaps are in four sections.

The flap actuators are in the fully extended position. A pair of 205 volt, three-phase ac motors, joined by differential gearing, make up the flap power unit; which is located in the fuselage to the rear of the rear wing spar.

The B-52H is powered by eight Pratt & Whitney TF-33-P-3 turbofan engines; which are mounted in pairs. They are numbered 1 through 8, from left to right. The first and second stage N-1 compressor blades are longer than the remaining blades; which results in cowlings that are noticeably different from the earlier turbojet powered B-52s. The T-33 develops 50% more takeoff thrust and 20% more cruise thrust than the J-57 engines; which previous B-52s used.

The larger forward cowlings allow fan bypass air to be discharged over the afterbody of the engine nacelles. There are eight auxiliary air inlet doors provided to assist in allowing ample airflow across the compressor inlet. These are springloaded to the closed position and are opened by differential air pressure.

The underside of the starboard wing, showing the Fowler flaps in the fully extended position. The interior of the flap well is Chromate Yellow.

The starboard wing tip has a ALT-32L Electronic Countermeasures (ECM) antenna concealed under the skin of the wingtip.

The starboard wingtip navigation light is Green; while the port wingtip light is Red.

The four section Fowler trailing edge flaps are identical on all models of the B-52.

The B-52G engine nacelle shape is noticeably different from the B-52H nacelle, and is one of the most identifiable differences between the two aircraft.

The B-52G is powered by eight Pratt & Whitney J-57-P-43WB turbojets with a maximum thrust of 13,759 pounds with water injection, and 11,200 pounds without water injection.

Both B-52G (left) and B-52H (right) carry non-jettisonable 700 gallon external underwing fuel tanks mounted outboard of the wingtip landing gear. The wing tip landing gear is identical on both variants.

This is the rear of the fairing for the ALCM launch pylons. It is mounted inboard of the inboard engine pylon. This fairing is wider and longer than those used to mount conventional bombs and/or the earlier air launched weapons carried by the B-52, such as the Hound Dog missile.

The inboard engine pylon of the B-52H mounts a pair of TF-33 turbofan engines. Bypass air exhausts from the rear portion of forward cowling, providing some thrust augmentation.

These are engine accessary exhaust vents. These vents are located on the inboard side of the engine nacelle.

One of the cooling air scoops located on the engine nacelle for engine mounted accessories.

The engine nacelle area between the engines, looking rearward. The complex curve of the rear of the engine pylon is visible

Engines 1, 3, 5, and 7 mount 120 KV generators on the lower port side, while engines 1, 3 4, 5, 6, and 7 mount engine driven variable delivery hydraulic pumps on the lower right side. All engines have cartridge start capability. These various accessories all require intake and exhaust venting.

The engine nacelle area between the TF-33 engines, looking forward. The forward cowling rings do not extend all the way around the afterbody cowl.

B-52 Wing

All B-52 models mount eight jet engines housed in pairs slung forward and under the wing. The engine nacelles varied depending on the power plant being used. The underwing pylon can be used to carry iron bombs or air-to-surface missiles depending on the mission requirements. Unlike the upper surface, there are no spoilers mounted on the wing undersurface.

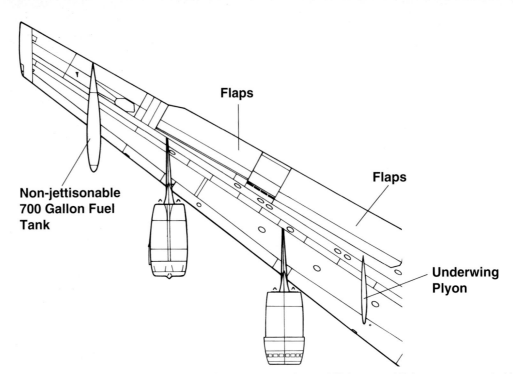

Non-jettisonable 700 Gallon Fuel Tank

Flaps

Flaps

Underwing Plyon

The internal wing structure is revealed by the extension of the inboard sections of the flaps. All plumbing and flight control linkages are mounted behind the wing rear spar, since the area between front and rear wing spars is occupied by fuel cells.

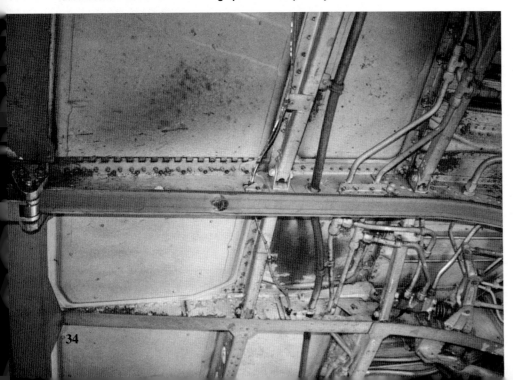

This is the wing (bottom) and fuselage (top) joint viewed from the underside of the wing.

This is an additional view of the wing interior structure that is revealed by the deployed flaps.

The interior wing ribs are made of aluminum, with aluminum or bonded magnesium wing skin attached to them. Corrosion control on the B-52 is especially important, since magnesium is extremely vulnerable to corrosion.

Four Lundy AN/ALE-24 chaff dispensers are located in the undersides of each wing, located between the inboard and outboard flap sections. The diffusion of the chaff packages is assured by the turbulence associated with aerodynamic forces in this area.

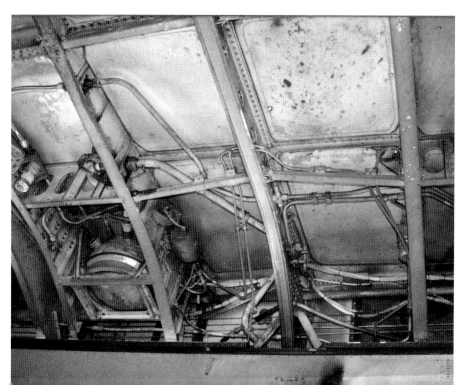

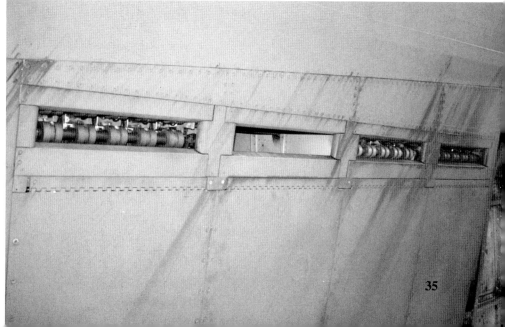

The inboard (above) and outboard (below) engine nacelles are virtually identical. The suck-in doors which surround the forward portion of the cowlings are closed. The suck-in doors on the TF-33 provide additional air at low speeds. They are spring loaded to the closed position (shown) and are only open at low speeds; while the engines are operating. They close gradually with increased speed.

This is a TF-33 turbofan engine mounted on a maintenance dolly. The engine accessory sections are in the middle of the engine.

This is the front of the TF-33 turbofan engine. The foremost fan blades are the low pressure compressor fan stages. The blade stages are well behind the fan stages, and are surrounded by the large shroud.

The engine mounted accessory units include the engine driven hydraulic pump, fuel pump, fuel control unit and starter.

The inlet of the TF-33 turbofan engine. The closed suck-in doors are just visible immediately forward of the low pressure compressor fan stages.

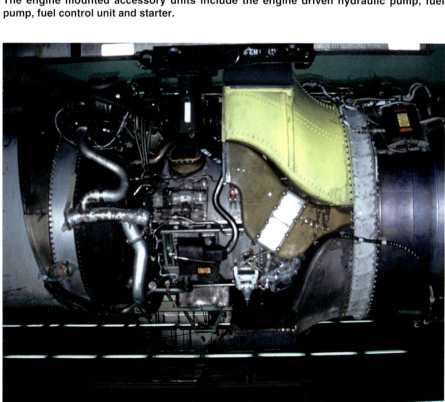

The engine oil tank is immediately to the rear of the fan air duct exit.

These are additional engine mounted accessories, including the accessory drive case.

B-52 models from the XB-52 to the B-52G used the J-57 turbojet engine. The B-52D used the J-57 PW-29, shown here with the nacelle lower access doors opened. These engine produced a maximum takeoff thrust of 12,100 pounds each. (USAF)

J-57 powered B-52Ds carried the brunt of the SAC war effort during the Vietnam War, including Arc Light and Linebacker missions. The upper access doors are held open by a rod at the front of the door. (USAF)

Groundcrews remove an engine for overhaul at Anderson AFB, Guam, during 1972. J-57 engines were upgraded from 10,500 pounds of thrust to 13,750 pounds of thrust (in the G model); with addition of increasing amounts of water injection. (USAF)

The four starboard J-57 engines of a NB-52B in flight. The B-52 had a very pronounced wing flex. The wing arced a total of thirty-two feet, sixteen feet upward and sixteen feet downward while in flight. (Boeing)

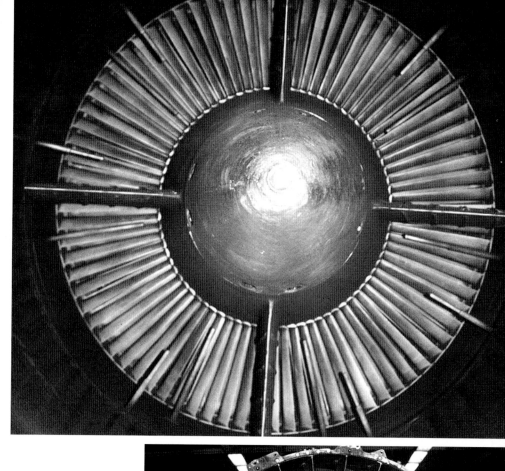

The Inboard nacelle of the TF-33 engines reveals the complex shape which terminates the fan exhaust rings.

(Right) This is the business end of the TF-33 turbofan engine, showing the 4th stage turbine blades.

This airscoop supplies cooling air to the engine accessory drive unit.

This is the front end of the TF-33 turbofan engine. The inlet guide vanes radiate from the nose dome and the low pressure fan stage blades are visible immediately behind the guide vanes.

The outrigger tip protection landing gear wheel well is located to the rear of the main wing spar.

(left) The port outrigger tip protection landing gear. This small wing mounted landing gear provides protection for the tip tanks under high gross weight takeoffs and landings.

The outrigger tip protection landing gear doors are in two sections. This is the inboard section; which covers the 20 x 4.4 inch wheel when the gear is retracted.

The outrigger tip protection landing gear wheel well is thirty-nine inches wide at the widest spot.

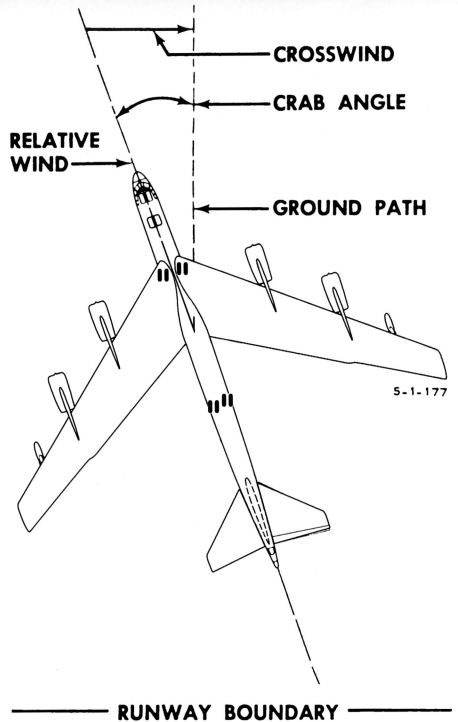

5-1-177

The port side of the forward main landing gear. One of the most interesting features of the B-52 landing gear (all models) is the ability of the pilots to adjust a crab angle into the gear, based on surface winds. This allows the B-52 to line up with the runway, while the fuselage remains pointed into the relative wind.

The rear main landing gear. The landing gear can be fully retracted in 10-15 seconds.

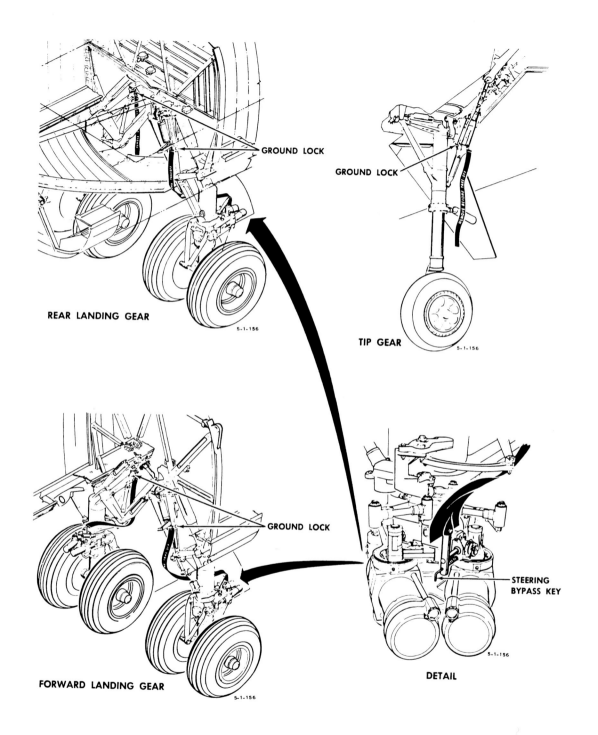

The forward section of the right rear main landing gear well. Oleo safety switches prevent accidental retraction of the main gear when the oleo is compressed more than 3/4 of an inch.

The main gear wheel wells are a complex maze of wires, hydraulic lines and control cables; which control extension, retraction, and crosswind landing and takeoff adjustment of the main landing gear.

Forward main landing gear. The crosswind landing adjustment feature of the landing gear means that the gear will always be lined up with the runway, while the fuselage may not be; which necessitates mounting the landing lights on the landing gear.

This view of the main gear shows additional details of the landing lights and the steering gear.

Preflighting the main landing gear, viewed from the rear. The extremely large size of the main landing gear is evident.

This is a portion of the main landing gear mount.

The main landing gear mount. The ground locks are Red-flagged Red pins inserted in the gear to assure that the gear cannot be retracted accidentally; while the aircraft is on the ground.

The main gear wheels are aluminum. They mount 56 x 16 38-ply tubeless tires. The weight of the main gear results in the main gear falling almost to the down and locked position after they are unlocked by hydraulic pressure.

This is the outrigger tip protection landing gear wheel and oleo.

Taxi lights are mounted on the main landing gear doors. Main gear steering is controlled by use of the rudder pedals with power supplied by individual hydraulic systems.

The right rear main landing gear, looking rearward. The main landing gears rotate 90° before retracting, in this case, to the rear.

Right rear main landing gear door, looking forward. The gear doors close inward after the gear retracts into the well. The forward gear retracts forward and the rear gear retracts to the rear.

Right rear main gear door. The indentations accommodate the main wheels and gear strut when the gear is retracted.

Right rear main landing gear wheel well details, showing the complex gear retraction and suspension systems. The safety pin prevents accidental retraction on the ground.

The left rear main landing gear well, looking forward. The left rear main landing gear retracts forward.

The right forward main landing gear well, looking forward.

A B-52H of the 5th Bomb Wing on final approach to Nellis Air Force Base, with the landing gear and flaps fully extended. (Ted Carlson Fotodynamics.)

Rear left main gear, looking forward. There are six emergency gear switches on the pilot's instrument panel; which control the extension of all six landing gears. The main gear can be extended or retracted, while the outrigger gears can only be extended under emergency power, which is provided by alternate hydraulic systems. Each gear can be actuated independently of the others.

The left forward main landing gear leg, looking rearward. The tubing on the left side of the strut are hydraulic lines for the steering and brakes.

49

The right side of the fuselage of a B-52H, showing the bomb bay bulkhead stiffeners (center and above).

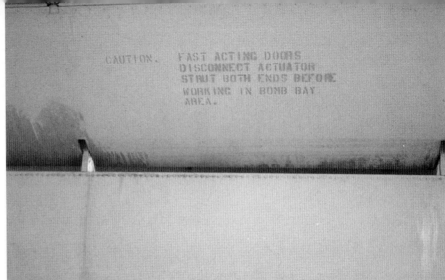

The bomb bay doors are so fast acting that the actuating rods are normally disconnected when the doors are open on the ground to avoid the possibility of serious injury to ground personnel in the case of accidental actuation. The warning lettering is in Red.

Six double-panel doors cover the bomb bay. All actuation of the bomb door system affects the lower doors only. The upper panels are hinged to provide a larger opening for ground servicing and loading only. The actuating rods (inverted "V") on the forward bulkhead are normally not connected on the ground.

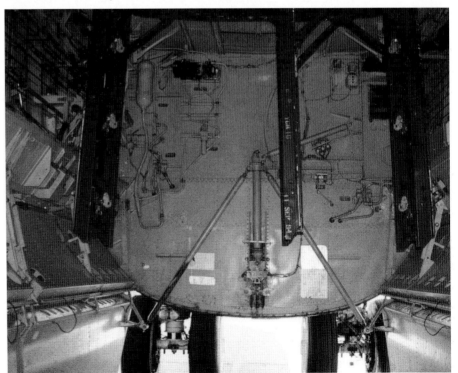

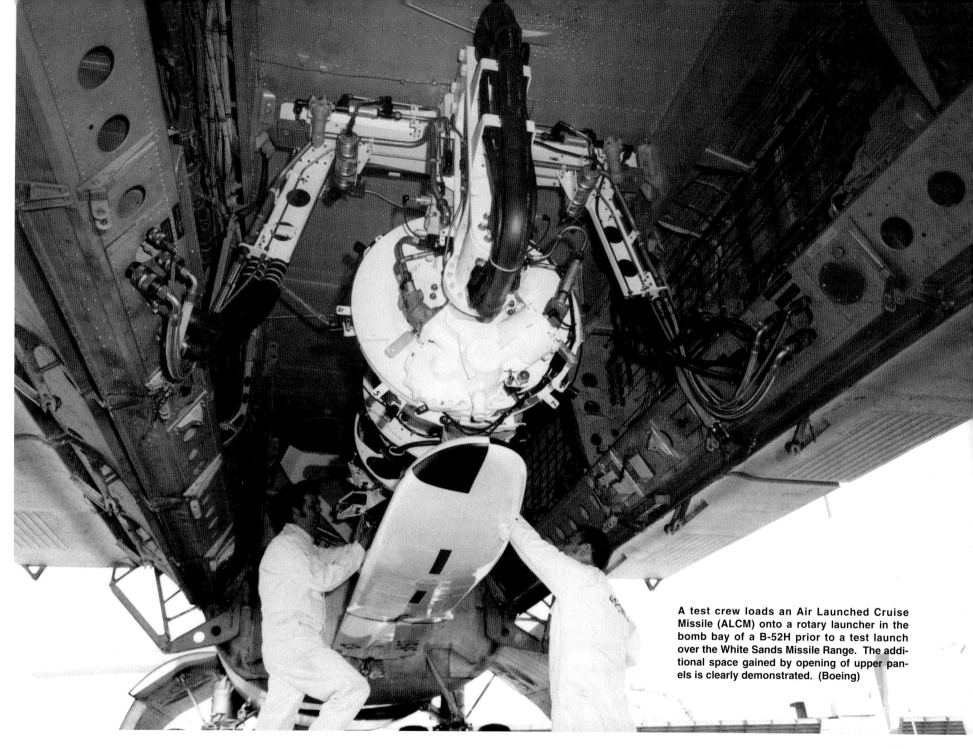

A test crew loads an Air Launched Cruise Missile (ALCM) onto a rotary launcher in the bomb bay of a B-52H prior to a test launch over the White Sands Missile Range. The additional space gained by opening of upper panels is clearly demonstrated. (Boeing)

The center bomb bay latching mechanism is located on the lower edge of the bulkhead. The bomb doors are held closed by these switches and held open by hydraulic pressure. The doors can be operated by the pilot or the radar navigator or automatically by the Bombing Navigation System (BNS).

These are the spring-loaded bomb release clips on one of the three conventional cluster bomb racks which can be loaded internally on the B-52. Each of these racks carries nine bombs.

The rear of the bomb bay, showing the guide which ensures that the fins of departing bombs do not swing to the side as they are released.

The upper bomb bay panel, with covered cannon plugs. These plugs are used to connect alternate bomb delivery systems.

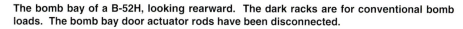

The bomb bay of a B-52H, looking rearward. The dark racks are for conventional bomb loads. The bomb bay door actuator rods have been disconnected.

(Above/Below) The bomb bays are lined with control cables, electrical bundles, and hydraulic system lines. The right body hydraulic system provides primary power to operate the doors, while the left body system acts as a backup. The holes in the beams are to lighten the structure as a weight saving measure.

(Top/Bottom/Right) The bomb doors are latched at the forward and rear bulkheads of the bomb bay. To secure simultaneous action of all doors, the center doors are mechanically linked to the forward and rear doors. The bomb jettison, GAM-72 launch gear jettison, and SWESS systems, will open the doors, but will not close them. The actuating rods on the forward bulkhead have been disconnected and are hanging down (below). A timer acts to close the doors automatically three seconds after the last bomb release pulse from the bomb release interval control.

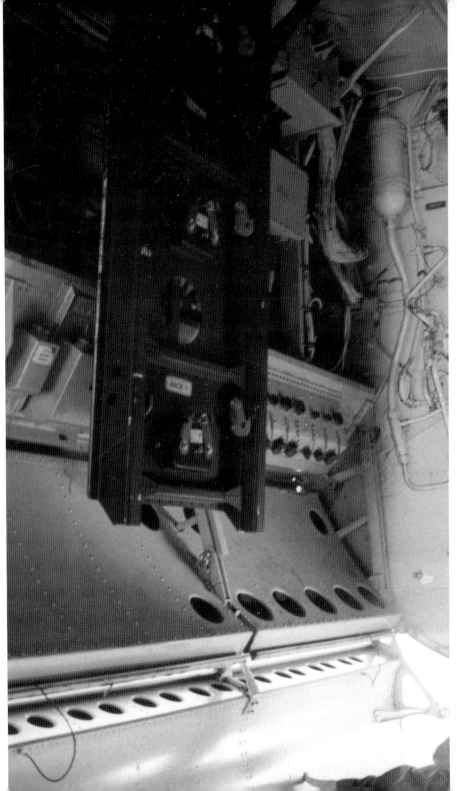

All early models of the B-52 mounted quad .50 caliber machine guns in the tail gun position. In the B-52A through the B-52F, the gunner's position was in the tail. The guns were radar directed. This B-52D also has ECM gear and tail warning radar. The drag chute door under the tail is open.

Maintenance on the quad fifties in the tail of a B-52. Each gun had 600 rounds of ammunition. The gunner had search, acquisition, and tracking modes on his radar. Tracking normally did not begin until the target was within 6,000 yards. In a gunfight, the B-52 had a chance. If the fighter used radar directed missiles, the BUFF was in trouble. (USAF)

The gunner's position in the B-52D. B-52 gunners were credited with shooting down two MIG-21s during the Linebacker II bombing campaign over North Vietnam, during December, 1972. Tail gunners did not enjoy the luxury of ejection seats. In the event of an emergency, they were to jettison the turret and jump. (Boeing)

The extended tail fairing of the B-52H. B-52s no longer carry guns or gunners, the logic being that modern fighters would not approach to within gun range before firing their missiles, and that Electronic Countermeasures (ECM) would be a more effective defensive measure.

The additional bulge on the underside of the extreme tail of this B-52H is one of the elements of the Phase VI Electronic Countermeasures (ECM) gear.

The B-52 stabilizer is all-moving, though stabilizer movement is for trim only. The primary pitch control is provided by the elevators on the trailing edges of the stabilizers. There are thirty-five vortex generators on the bottom of the stabilizer; which enhance the effectiveness of the elevators.

The horizontal stabilizer tip of a B-52H houses a pair of button antennas on the rear portion just in front of the elevator hinge line.

Three of the ECM blade antennas; which are mounted under the rear fuselage of the B-52H.

The 20MM Vulcan six-barrel cannon has been removed from the tail of the B-52H, but the ECM gear remains, including the ALR-46/ALZ-117 radome (the large bulge under the tail) and the ALQ-172 antenna (under the lower fire control radome). The large bulges just above the stabilizer are ALQ-117 antennas.

B-52s carry a stencil style Gray outline national insignia as part of their overall toned-down camouflage.

The square patches under the stabilizer of the B-52 are the covers over the chaff dispensers; which are part of the ECM equipment package.

The faired cooling air exhaust vents service the aft equipment bay. The Red safety ribbon is attached to the latch for the aft equipment bay door.

These blade antennas on the fuselage sides are recognition features of the B-52H, mandated by the START treaty with the former Soviet Union.

The bulge just to the rear of the stabilizer is the I/J-band horn (ALR-20A, TN-391A Aft). They are on both sides of the fuselage.

The B-52G tail is markedly different from that of the B-52H, retaining the quad .50 M3 machine gun mount with the ASG-15 search radar.

The tail of a B-52H. The large bulge on the vertical fin is the AN/ALQ-153 ECM antenna. Other antennas on the B-52H vertical tail include the ARN-14 Omnirange, APN-69 radar beacon, and ARC-58 liaison radio antenna.

B-52G tail contains the same antennas as carried on the B-52H; while retaining the .50 caliber machine gun mount.

The B-52G gunner's crew station is aft-facing in the forward fuselage, next to the Electronic Warfare Officer (EWO). The CRT immediately in front of the gunner is the TV monitor.

The pilot's ejection seat in the B-52H. The pilot and co-pilot seats both eject upward. The arming levers for the seats are contained in each armrest. A series of ballistic devices and mechanical linkages incorporated in the seat, when initiated by either arming lever, will lock the inertia reel, stow the control column, jettison the hatch, and arm the seat for ejection. Each seat can be adjusted up, down, forward, aft, and tilted. A warning in the manual states that using any cushion other than what is provided may cause serious injury during ejection.

The B-52 control wheel contains controls for stabilizer and lateral trim, autopilot, air refueling (IFR) boom release and the interphone-mike trigger switch.

The current instrument panel of the B-52H is dominated by the Electro-optical Viewing System (EVS) monitor. The EVS presents a "TV" picture, generated by either the STV or FLIR systems.

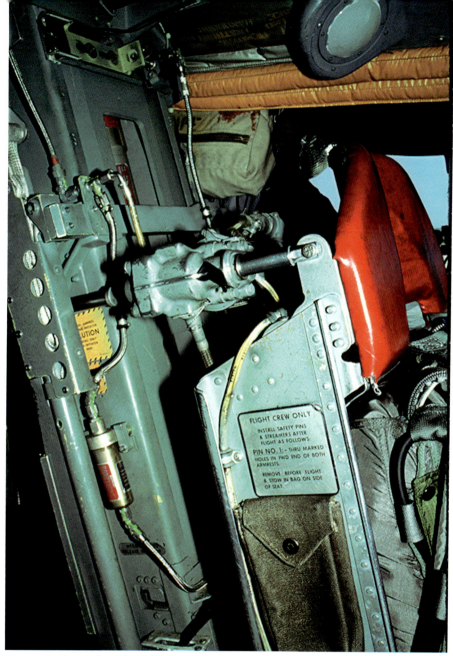

The pocket located on the side of the ejection seat is for the storage for the seat safeing pins.

(Right) The center console is dominated by the eight throttles. Other significant features include the crosswind landing adjustment knob at the rear of the console, and the drag chute lever on the co-pilots side of the console.

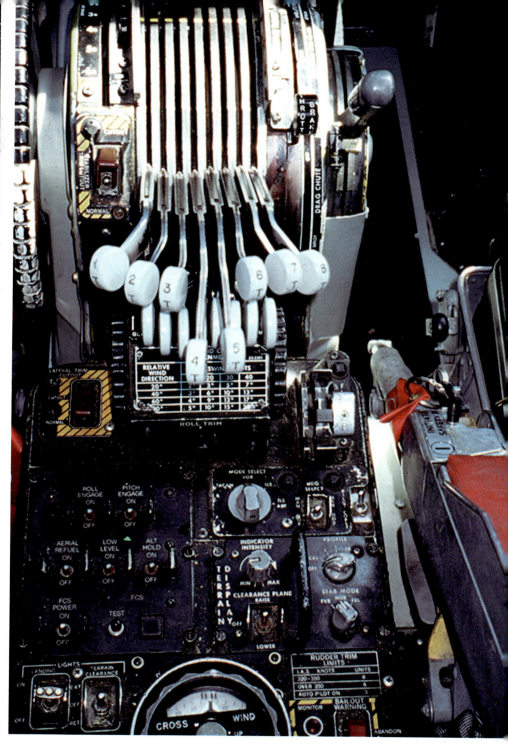

Crew Positions

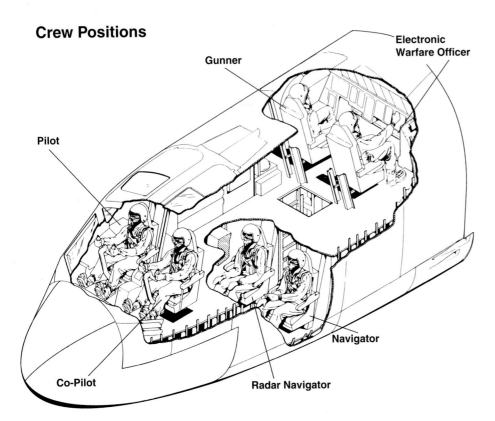

B-52G and B-52H crew station arrangement. The gunner (seated on the starboard side, facing aft) has been removed from the B-52H crew; since the B-52H no longer carries any guns.

The B-52 flight manual states that *"under level flight conditions, eject at least 2,000 feet above the terrain whenever possible."* It also states that, *"under spin or dive conditions, eject at least 15,000 feet above the terrain whenever possible."* According to the manual, accident statistics show a progressive decrease in successful ejections as altitude decreases below 2,000 feet above the terrain. The ejection check list calls for the pilot to reduce airspeed, trim for level flight and engage the autopilot. If at extremely low level, it is recommended that the nose be pulled up into a "zoom" maneuver, to give more time for parachute deployment. The navigator is ejected first to make his hatch available for use in the event of a seat failure and to allow any extra crew to use this hatch. The pilot is the last to eject, after ensuring all other crew have left the aircraft.

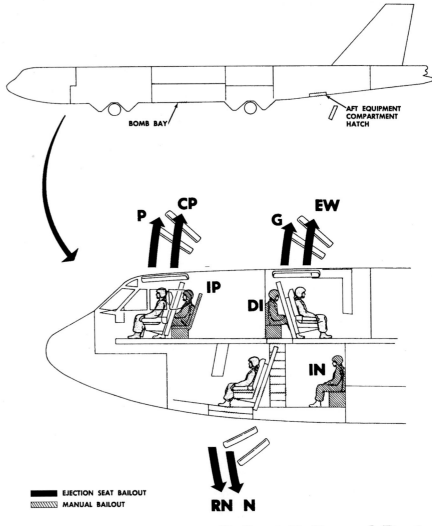

Bailout Exits and Routes

Any extra crew on board, such as instructor pilot's, instruction navigators, and defensive systems instructors, would have to bailout manually after the crew ejects.

The B-52H instrument panels include vintage analog instruments as well as the state-of-the-art EVS monitors. Engine instruments are clustered in the center of the panel.

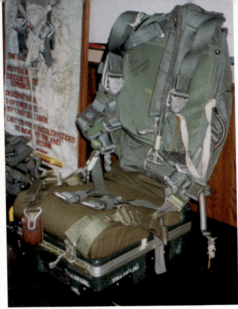

B-52H parachute and survival seat kit are integral. The Yellow handle on the right side of the seat lowers the seat pack on a lanyard to hang below the crewman before making a parachute landing.

The parachute and survival package separates (along with it's occupant) from the ejection seat one second after firing of the seat.

The Radar Navigator's panel has kept up with navigation advances, and now includes an integrated keyboard and a pair of Multi-function Displays.

The view to the rear from the Navigator's compartment. The Yellow "egg crate" is a fold-down panel; which covers the crew access hatch. The hatch leading aft is open and immediately below that hatch is the seat for the Instructor Navigator (when carried).

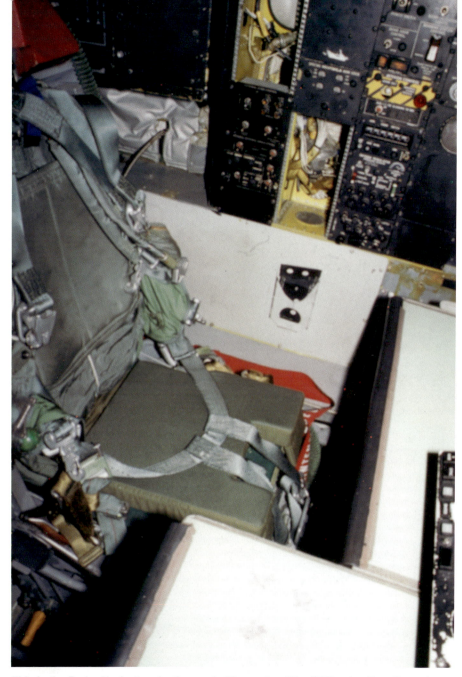

This is the Radar Navigator ejection seat. The seats of the "Offensive Team" are downward firing. Arming the seat for ejection will lock the inertial reel, stow the writing table, jettison the hatch, and lock the ankle restraints.

The overhead panel for the Radar Navigator includes manual releases for front and rear "Special Weapons" (i.e. Nukes).

A B-52H Radar Navigator of the 410th Bomb Wing at work. This is the crewman with primary responsibility for management of the B-52's offensive weapons.

This is the Instructor Navigators seat (when a IN is carried). The seat is located right next to the urinal.

The Navigator at work. The panel in front of the Navigator contains both flight instruments and weapons monitoring instruments.

Radar Navigators side instrument panel. Missing are the Coded Switch Panel and the Presentation Adjust Panel.

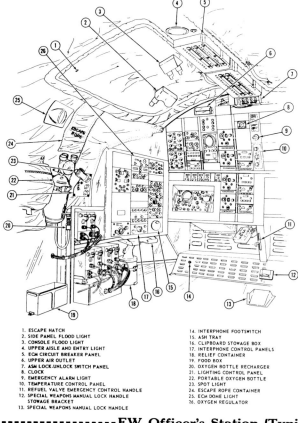

1. ESCAPE HATCH
2. SIDE PANEL FLOOD LIGHT
3. CONSOLE FLOOD LIGHT
4. UPPER AISLE AND ENTRY LIGHT
5. ECM CIRCUIT BREAKER PANEL
6. UPPER AIR OUTLET
7. ASM LOCK-UNLOCK SWITCH PANEL
8. CLOCK
9. EMERGENCY ALARM LIGHT
10. TEMPERATURE CONTROL PANEL
11. REFUEL VALVE EMERGENCY CONTROL HANDLE
12. SPECIAL WEAPONS MANUAL LOCK HANDLE STOWAGE BRACKET
13. SPECIAL WEAPONS MANUAL LOCK HANDLE
14. INTERPHONE FOOTSWITCH
15. ASH TRAY
16. CLIPBOARD STOWAGE BOX
17. INTERPHONE CONTROL PANELS
18. RELIEF CONTAINER
19. FOOD BOX
20. OXYGEN BOTTLE RECHARGER
21. LIGHTING CONTROL PANEL
22. PORTABLE OXYGEN BOTTLE
23. SPOT LIGHT
24. ESCAPE ROPE CONTAINER
25. ECM DOME LIGHT
26. OXYGEN REGULATOR

▪▪▪▪▪▪▪▪▪▪▪▪▪▪▪▪▪▪▪▪EW Officer's Station (Typical)

The gunners station retains many of the instrumentation, including the RHAW threat presentation scope. Missing are the controls for the gun

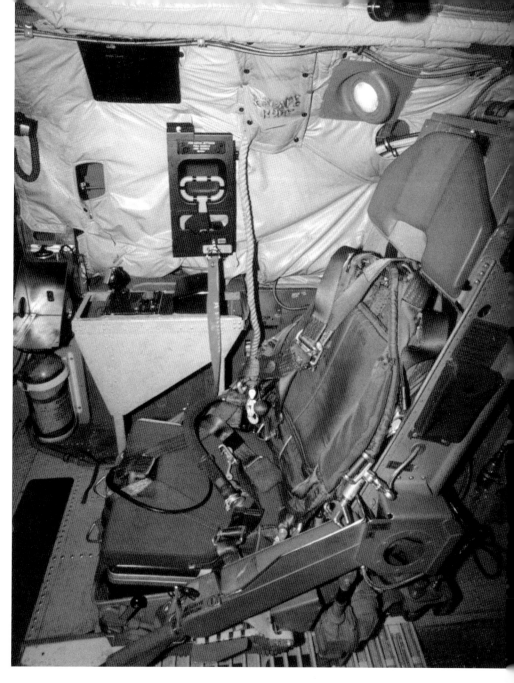

The gunner's ejection seat. The striped handle on the cabin wall is the hatch jettison handle (the stowed rope immediately to the rear of the handle is used to lower yourself from the hatch, which is on top of the fuselage, to the ground.)

The overhead panel contains, from top to bottom: Overhead lighting panel, standby UHF Command radio panel, UHF Command Radio Control Panel, TACAN Radio, Omni-Range radio, and the air refueling panel.

The yellow striped switches are jettison switches for, top to bottom: GAM-72, Bomb Bay, and ASM Jettison Controls.

The oxygen system control panel is at the rear end of the overhead panel.

The eyebrow instrument panel contains oil pressure gages (left and right), accelerometer, standby magnetic compass, cabin altitude gage, and air refueling lights

The forward section of the co-pilot's right hand console contains the AC control panel, DC control panel, and interphone panel.

The rear portion of the right hand console provides a storage location for manuals and charts.

The middle of the right hand console contains circuit breakers, HF radio controls, Oxygen system controls, and the emergency DC power panel.

The hatch behind the Instructor Pilots seat leads to the Navigator's compartment and out through the belly of the airplane. The Yellow "eggcrate" covers the opening when not in use.

69

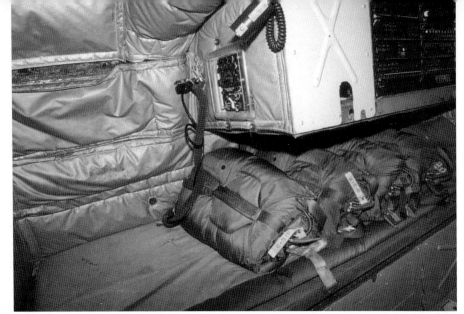

The area behind the co-pilots seat includes a large circuit breaker panel.

The co-pilot's panel and side console. The entire lower half of the panel, from the right side of the center console to the right side console, is devoted to the management of the fuel system.

The area behind the Instructor Pilot's seat features a crew rest cot (being used to store additional parachutes for those unlucky enough to have to bail out without benefit of an ejection seat). All instructors and other non-crew riders must bail out manually.

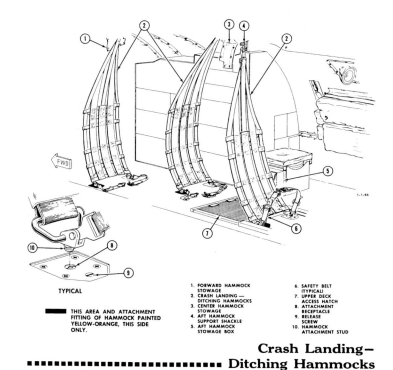

TYPICAL

■ THIS AREA AND ATTACHMENT FITTING OF HAMMOCK PAINTED YELLOW-ORANGE, THIS SIDE ONLY.

1. FORWARD HAMMOCK STOWAGE
2. CRASH LANDING—DITCHING HAMMOCKS
3. CENTER HAMMOCK STOWAGE
4. AFT HAMMOCK SUPPORT SHACKLE
5. AFT HAMMOCK STOWAGE BOX
6. SAFETY BELT (TYPICAL)
7. UPPER DECK ACCESS HATCH
8. ATTACHMENT RECEPTACLE
9. RELEASE SCREW
10. HAMMOCK ATTACHMENT STUD

Crash Landing— Ditching Hammocks

The view forward, at floor level, from the crew access hatch, showing the IP seat and pilot's seat.

(Right) The B-52H Defense Instructor sits on a chemical toilet during much of the flight. (it is equipped with a seat belt and oxygen/radio leads.)

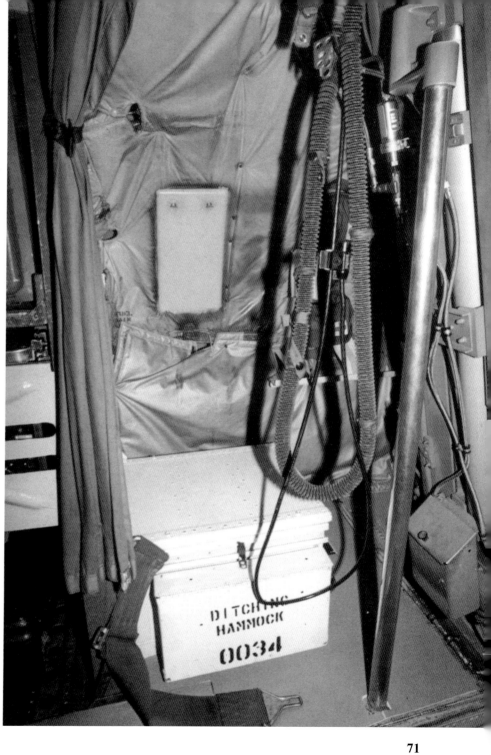

The sextant is normally kept in this carrying case when not in use.

This circuit breaker panel is located just behind and to the side of the navigators station.

Even with the routine usage of satellite-based Global Positioning System (GPS) equipment and Inertial Navigation Systems, the navigator still has the option to use a sextant to shoot sun and star positions to determine the B-52's location.

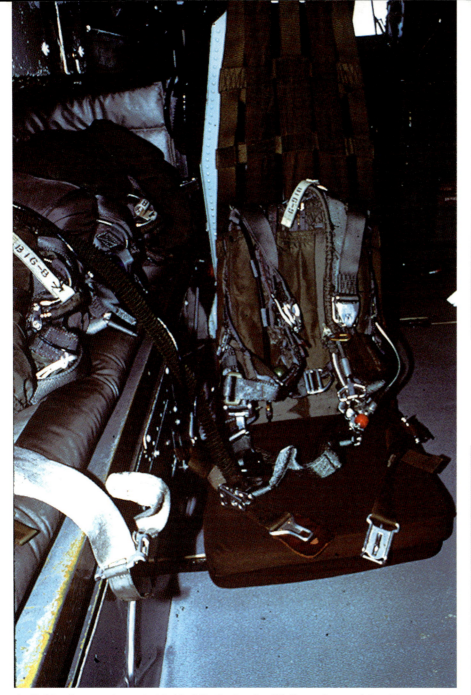

A ditching hammock erected behind the Instructor Pilot's seat, complete with parachute and seat cushion survival pack.

The oxygen regulator and interphone control panel is located just above the crew bunk.

A B-52 pilot's helmet with Night Vision Goggles (NVG) installed. A recent addition to the B-52, the NVGs are worn on low level night missions, where they are more effective than FLIR or EVS systems, since they allow the pilot to scan the terrain to either side of the flight line.

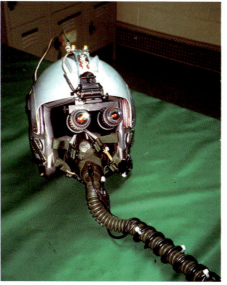
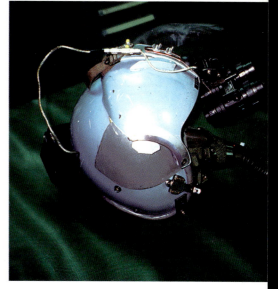

The B-52 was used as a tactical bomber during the first seven years of the Vietnam War. "Arc Light" missions were flown against suspected and/or confirmed enemy staging areas or fortified positions where the B-52's awesome conventional weapons capability had a devastating effect on area targets. (USAF)

B-52s were first used against Vietnam in 1965, in the pre-camouflage era. They were based at Anderson AFB, Guam, 2,200 miles from their targets. 750 pound bombs are loaded on the underwing rack. The B-52D carried a total of forty-two of these bombs internally and twelve on each of the underwing pylons originally designed for carriage of the Hound Dog missile. (USAF)

An armorer prepares to haul another load of 500 pound bombs to B-52s during Operation Linebacker II, the late 1972 strategic campaign against North Vietnam; which led to the end of U.S. involvement in the Vietnam war. The B-52D carried 108 of these bombs and was able to deliver them with great accuracy. (USAF)

B-52s were armed with the first of the air-launched stand-off weapons, the AGM-28 Hound Dog. The Hound Dog was powered by a 7,500 lbst J-52 engine and since it's launch pylon was connected to the B-52's fuel tanks, it's engine could be used by the B-52 to augment thrust. Once launched, the AGM-28 could attain Mach 2 speeds for ranges up to 700 miles, depending upon launch altitude. It carried a 1,675 pound W-28 warhead of one megaton yield. Hound Dogs stood alert from 1959 to 1976.

Members of the 68th Munitions Maintenance Squadron prepare to load simulated B-28 nuclear bombs aboard a B-52G of the 68th Bomb Wing at Barksdale AFB during a 1974 SAC Weapons Loading Competition. The B-28 was the nuclear weapon manufactured in largest numbers. Yields varied from 70 kilotons to 1.45 megatons. (USAF)

Sixty-nine of the 167 B-52Gs; which were operational during 1991 were fitted for the force projection role (i.e delivery of conventional weapons) using the Integrated Conventional Stores-Management System. This is an external load of 500 pound bombs on B-52G (serial 59-588), at March AFB on 7 November 1992. (Ted Carlson-Fotodynamics)

Nearly twenty years after Vietnam, the B-52 was still flying tactical missions against enemy positions, this time in the Persian Gulf. A B-52G takes off for a mission against elements of the Iraqi Republican Guard during Operation DESERT STORM in January of 1991. (USAF)

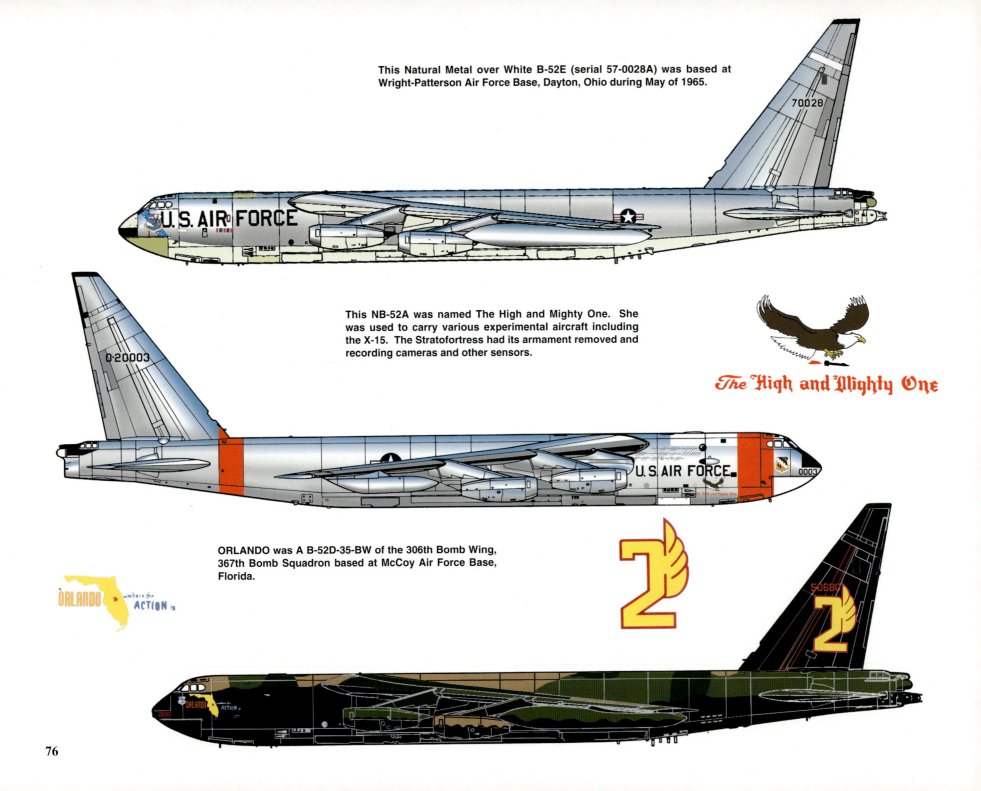

This Natural Metal over White B-52E (serial 57-0028A) was based at Wright-Patterson Air Force Base, Dayton, Ohio during May of 1965.

This NB-52A was named The High and Mighty One. She was used to carry various experimental aircraft including the X-15. The Stratofortress had its armament removed and recording cameras and other sensors.

ORLANDO was A B-52D-35-BW of the 306th Bomb Wing, 367th Bomb Squadron based at McCoy Air Force Base, Florida.

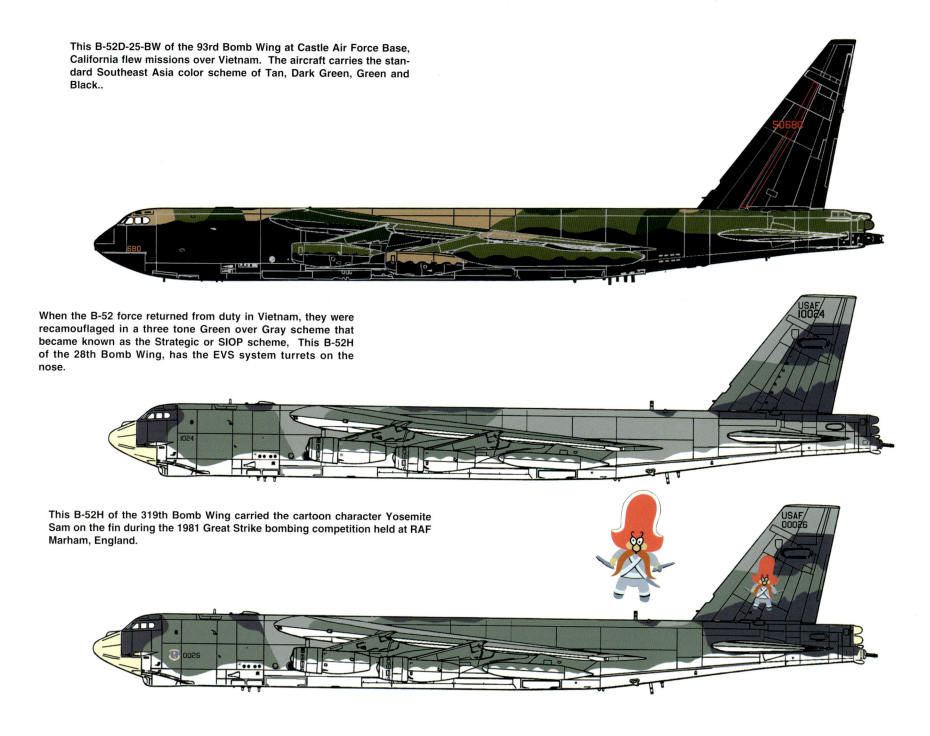

This B-52D-25-BW of the 93rd Bomb Wing at Castle Air Force Base, California flew missions over Vietnam. The aircraft carries the standard Southeast Asia color scheme of Tan, Dark Green, Green and Black..

When the B-52 force returned from duty in Vietnam, they were recamouflaged in a three tone Green over Gray scheme that became known as the Strategic or SIOP scheme, This B-52H of the 28th Bomb Wing, has the EVS system turrets on the nose.

This B-52H of the 319th Bomb Wing carried the cartoon character Yosemite Sam on the fin during the 1981 Great Strike bombing competition held at RAF Marham, England.

A B-52G armed with AGM-86 Air Launched Cruise Missiles (ALCMs). The AGM-86B is the nuclear armed variant, carrying a 200 kiloton warhead at subsonic speed over a range of 1,500 miles.

A B-52H armed with AGM-69A missiles. 1,500 AGM-69s were manufactured to equip eighteen SAC bases by 1975. The B-52 could carry up to twenty of these missiles (twelve externally and eight on a rotary launcher in the bomb bay); which had a yield of 200 kilotons. AGM-69 had a top speed of up to Mach 3.2 and a range; which varied (according to launch altitude) from thirty-five to 105 miles. Its guidance was inertial. (USAF)

The NB-52B had a long and varied career, carrying a wide assortment of NASA test vehicles aloft and launching them over Edwards Air Force Base, California. It is carrying the X-24B Lifting Body, one of the test aircraft that proved the viability of the Space Shuttle concept. (NASA)

The Pegasus was carried in tests by the NB-52B. The Pegasus was launched at 40,000 feet, and could carry a 900 pound payload into low earth orbit. It is forty-nine feet long, fifty inches in diameter and weighs 41,000 pounds. (Ted Carlson-Fotodynamics)

A B-52H of the 410th Bomb Wing being loaded with AGM-129A Advanced Air Launched Cruise Missiles (ALCMs). The AGM-129A is a stealth-engineered follow-on to the AGM-86 ALCM.

The B-52H was fitted with a stub pylon mounted between the inboard and outboard engine pylons to carry a Sidewinder air-to-air missile launch rail. During training exercises, an ACMI pod is carried on this rail.

The AGM-129A has folding wings and tail fins. It is powered by a turbojet engine and is subsonic, with guidance provided by TERCOM and GPS, using a radar altimeter to provide minimum ground clearance. According to the USAF, one of these loaded pylons weighs as much, costs as much, and is as complex as an F-16A fighter. The AGM-129A weighs 2,750 pounds and has a range of 1,800 nautical miles. It is nuclear or conventional warhead-capable.

A B-52H takes off with a load of ALCMs. The AGM-129A resembles it's predecessor, the AGM-86. Thirty-five Conventional warhead AGM-86C ALCMs were fired against Iraqi targets during Operation DESERT STORM. These missions were flown by Barksdale-based B-52Gs; which meant mission times in excess of thirty-four hours!

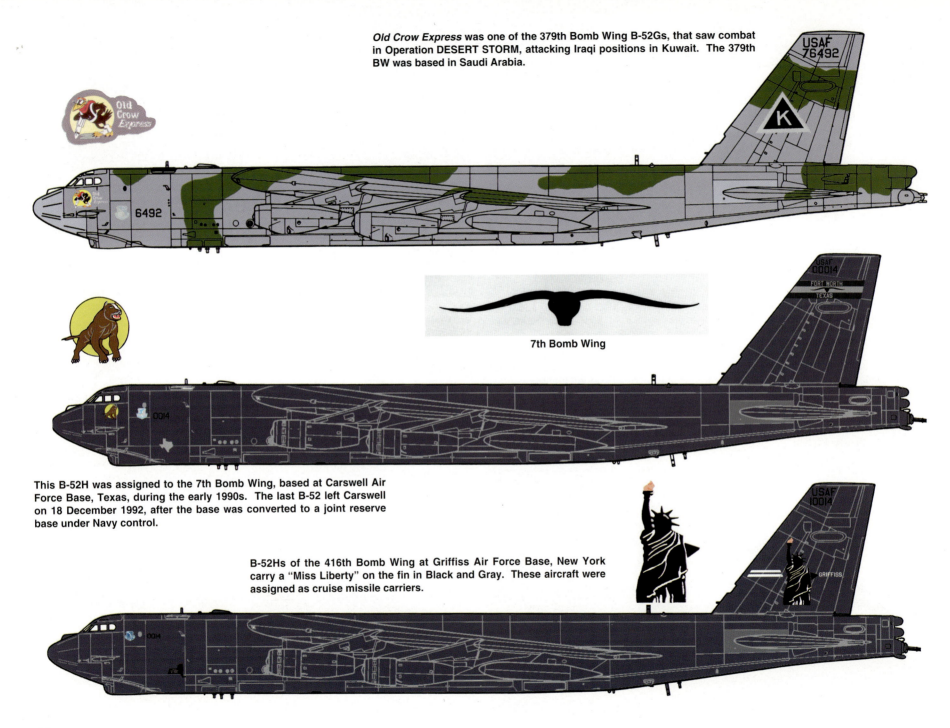

Old Crow Express was one of the 379th Bomb Wing B-52Gs, that saw combat in Operation DESERT STORM, attacking Iraqi positions in Kuwait. The 379th BW was based in Saudi Arabia.

7th Bomb Wing

This B-52H was assigned to the 7th Bomb Wing, based at Carswell Air Force Base, Texas, during the early 1990s. The last B-52 left Carswell on 18 December 1992, after the base was converted to a joint reserve base under Navy control.

B-52Hs of the 416th Bomb Wing at Griffiss Air Force Base, New York carry a "Miss Liberty" on the fin in Black and Gray. These aircraft were assigned as cruise missile carriers.